OUT OF THE WATER

WATER

Brooke Berman

BROADWAY PLAY PUBLISHING INC
224 E 62nd St, NY, NY 10065
www.broadwayplaypub.com
info@broadwayplaypub.com

OUT OF THE WATER
© Copyright 2012 by Brooke Berman

First printing: November 2012
Second printing: November 2013
I S B N: 978-0-88145-546-5

Book design: Marie Donovan
Page make-up: Adobe Indesign
Typeface: Palatino
Printed and bound in the U S A

CHARACTERS & SETTING

POLLY, *30s, a jaded New Yorker*
GRAHAM, *40s, her ex-stepbrother. A jaded Midwesterner*
CAT, *17, a wide-eyed innocent and savvy traveler*

Time: Now

Place: Libertyville, IL, and New York, NY

Scene: Do you remember me?

(A funeral home in the Midwest. POLLY *enters, nervously, looks around. She is dressed like a New Yorker, some combination of Chrissy Hynde and Carrie Bradshaw.* GRAHAM *approaches. She has no idea who he is.)*

GRAHAM: Do you remember me?

POLLY: No. I'm sorry. Should I?

GRAHAM: You don't remember me?

POLLY: Were you a friend of his?

GRAHAM: I was not a friend of his.

POLLY: Tell me who you are?

GRAHAM: Try harder.

POLLY: I'm sorry, you're going to have to excuse me, I'm—

GRAHAM: //Yes?

POLLY: I'm only here because my mother can't be. I'm not a relative.

GRAHAM: I know.

POLLY: And I don't have many happy memories.

GRAHAM: At all?

POLLY: Oh. No, I have happy memories. Just not of this particular town. Or my mom's married life. Or him. I haven't been back to Libertyville, Illinois, in—

GRAHAM: Fifteen years.

POLLY: Tell me who you are.

GRAHAM: No. This is fun.

POLLY: This isn't fun. You're kind of creeping me out right now in this really major way, and, it was great talking to you, but I should go.

GRAHAM: Graham. I'm Graham.

POLLY: Oh. *(This knocks her out.)* Oh. I'm sorry. I'm so, so—so sorry. I just didn't expect—I mean I know that sounds awful, he's your *dad*, of course you'd be here, but—I kind of forgot you existed.

GRAHAM: *(Not insulted)* It's been a long time.

POLLY: How are you? Are you okay?

GRAHAM: I'm okay.

POLLY: Your wife? Is she here?

GRAHAM: Anita. She's not here.

POLLY: Oh.

GRAHAM: She's home with the kids.

POLLY: Oh.

GRAHAM: She did all this, planned it and everything. But then, she didn't come. Didn't even let the kids come. We had a big fight about it. She won.

POLLY: Oh.

GRAHAM: You say that a lot. "Oh."

POLLY: Well. I guess I don't know what to say. It's been a long time, Graham. And—

GRAHAM: We never—

POLLY: —Liked each other. No. we didn't. *(Beat)* I'm sorry for your loss.

GRAHAM: Thanks. I'm sorry for yours.

POLLY: Oh. It's not a loss for me. I keep trying to pretend it is one. But it isn't. When my mom married your dad, I guess he should have been some kind of parent, but—

GRAHAM: He wasn't cut out for parenting.

POLLY: No. He was not. Do you want to—?

GRAHAM: Yes.

POLLY: What?

GRAHAM: Get a drink. Get out of here. Anything. Please.

POLLY: I have a car outside. A rental.

GRAHAM: I have a car. I'll drive.

POLLY: No, really, I would prefer to have my own—

GRAHAM: You won't find the place. There's this place I like. You won't find it.

POLLY: I can find it.

GRAHAM: It's in Mundelein. Do you know Mundelein? I'll drive.

(POLLY *hesitates*)

GRAHAM: Come on.

(GRAHAM *ushers* POLLY *out—then—*)

POLLY: Wait. Can I see him one more time?

(GRAHAM *nods. Yes.* POLLY *goes into the room with the dead body. He waits for her. She's there a while. She comes back out. She nods. They quickly leave.*)

Scene: A bar in Mundelein. Do you know Mundelein?

GRAHAM: It wasn't easy. We did what we could. Anita was a saint.

POLLY: Cancer, right? Was it cancer?

GRAHAM: Anita was a saint. Nobody liked him, not until the end. Except my kids, my kids liked him. It's hard to really not like your grandparent. They so innocuous once they're grandparents. But me… *(He shrugs.)*

POLLY: I remember.

GRAHAM: Anita and I were left to take care of him. We didn't want to.

POLLY: But you did.

GRAHAM: It's just what you do.

POLLY: You hated him.

GRAHAM: We don't use that word in my family.

(POLLY *shoots* GRAHAM *one of those looks that says, Really!?*

GRAHAM: Okay. I hated him. But I took care of him at the end. Because it is just what you do.

POLLY: I don't.

GRAHAM: What?

POLLY: Do that.

GRAHAM: It was good for the kids. Kids need grandparents.

POLLY: I'm sure.

GRAHAM: You have kids?

POLLY: No.

GRAHAM: That's too bad.

POLLY: I don't know.

GRAHAM: You married?

(POLLY *shakes her head no…*)

GRAHAM: Ever been married?

(*Again,* POLLY *shakes her head no.*)

GRAHAM: That's too bad.

POLLY: It's fine.

GRAHAM: Family matters.

POLLY: So I hear.

GRAHAM: Why aren't you married? Are you like, um—?

POLLY: Am I like-um what?

GRAHAM: You know.

POLLY: I don't know why I'm not married. I'm not "like um" anything. I just, I don't know why I'm not.

GRAHAM: Okay.

POLLY: It's not my fault.

GRAHAM: I didn't say it was.

POLLY: I'm not sure what I want.

GRAHAM: What does that mean?

POLLY: It means I'm not sure what I want.

GRAHAM: You want kids?

POLLY: I don't know.

GRAHAM: You're too old to not know. You get like, how old are you? Thirty-four? Thirty-five? I mean, not to be a dick or anything, but it's harder after forty. On you, on the kid. There are all these statistics. So if you don't know—and you don't have any prospects— you've got like a few good years left to figure that out.

POLLY: Thanks, Graham. But I'm not so convinced about family. I know you say it matters, and maybe it does, but I think family is what gets us into trouble. Family, tribe, country. Anything that keeps us loyal to the pack—

GRAHAM: What "pack"?

POLLY: —like animals, like wolves. Or cows. We're better off alone. *(Small beat)* I could adopt.

GRAHAM: *(Giving her some shit for this)* You'd adopt.

POLLY: There are a lot of motherless children.

GRAHAM: Besides you and me?

POLLY: Yes. Besides you and me. There are babies and young children who need someone.

GRAHAM: Like from China?

POLLY: Like from anywhere. There are motherless children everywhere.

GRAHAM: You're not convinced about family. And you don't know if you want kids. But if you want one, you'll adopt it from China.

POLLY: Movie stars do it all the time.

GRAHAM: You're funny. You're gonna adopt a baby from— Listen, most girls I know—

POLLY: Women. I'm over thirty. I get to be called—

GRAHAM: Sure whatever. But most girls were dying to get married.

POLLY: I was dying to get out.

GRAHAM: Out of what?

POLLY: Out of here.

(Beat)

GRAHAM: Yeah. I was too.

POLLY: We hated each other.

GRAHAM: We don't use that word.

POLLY: But it wasn't personal. You know that, right? Hating you was never personal.

GRAHAM: Oh yeah. Me too. Yeah.

POLLY: Are you happy? I mean, in your "life"?

GRAHAM: Sure.

POLLY: Anita's good?

GRAHAM: She's great.

POLLY: Your kids?

GRAHAM: They're all good. We have three. You remember my daughter. She's in high school now. You remember her?

POLLY: Oh. Yes. I remember—I held her. When she was born. I held her and made up stories and whispered to her about—all the things she could look forward to. Boyfriends and music and lipstick, there was this lipstick, L'Oreal, galactic something—"Galactic Ice".

GRAHAM: I don't think she remembers that.

POLLY: Catherine. Right? Isn't it Catherine?

GRAHAM: Catherine Amanda. Like someone from a fucking book.

POLLY: That's nice.

GRAHAM: Her mom's idea. She goes by Cat now. She's seventeen. Girls love to name themselves after animals. Have you noticed? Cat? Bunny? Kitty? Bambi? What kind of parent lets his kid call herself "Bambi"?

POLLY: Personally, I always distrust girls named after animals.

GRAHAM: It's better than girls named after rocks. Some of her classmates, these girls she goes to school with, they have these names... Jade. Amber. Onyx. And in Ohio. What kind of ONYX lives in Ohio?

POLLY: Got it.

GRAHAM: What do you do? I mean, with your—you know, job?

POLLY: I own a bar.

GRAHAM: Really?

POLLY: Your dad taught me to hold my liquor.

GRAHAM: You go to school for that?

POLLY: I have a masters in European history.

GRAHAM: Really? *(Some cool appraisal goes on)* I never really knew you.

POLLY: You were older.

GRAHAM: You were afraid of me.

POLLY: I was not afraid of you. I am afraid of no one.

GRAHAM: As an eleven-year-old girl in that house in Libertyville, you were afraid of me.

POLLY: I don't remember that.

GRAHAM: I do.

POLLY: We just didn't get along. And then—

GRAHAM: They got divorced.

POLLY: Thank God.

GRAHAM: Who are we? To each other?

POLLY: Strangers.

GRAHAM: We're not strangers. We shared something.

POLLY: We didn't share anything.

GRAHAM: Sure we did.

POLLY: Maybe you shared something, but I didn't share anything. They were married for five minutes and you were older and they got divorced and nobody kept in touch. We did not share anything. There was nothing to share.

GRAHAM: How's your mother?

POLLY: Dead.

GRAHAM: Oh.

POLLY: I did not go back. To do what you did, take care of her. I know you said it's "what people do," —but it is not what I did.

GRAHAM: Oh.

POLLY: See what I mean about that word? Only I don't think you used it properly.

GRAHAM: Oh.

POLLY: Better.

(GRAHAM *and* POLLY *lock eyes.*)

POLLY: Are you attracted to me? You keep looking at my body.

GRAHAM: Well. We are strangers.

POLLY: You said we weren't.

GRAHAM: You said we were.

POLLY: Don't look at my body like that.

GRAHAM: Why?

(POLLY *leans over the table and kisses* GRAHAM *hard.*
That's why, Asshole. He reaches for her, and it's all over.
Kissing all the while, they move to the car—)

Scene: You can be adulterous in a rental car

(GRAHAM *and* POLLY, *post-coitus, in the rental car*)

POLLY: I can't believe you made us drive all the way back to my car.

GRAHAM: It's a rental. You can be adulterous in a rental.

POLLY: But not The Family Car.

GRAHAM: That's right.

(POLLY *shoots* GRAHAM *a look.*)

GRAHAM: Don't look at me like that. It's the family car. You have to consider The Family in the family car. Carpools. Church youth group. I can't have all kinds of—

POLLY: Cum-stains.

GRAHAM: Exactly.

POLLY: I'm family. You can have me in the family car.

GRAHAM: Not like this I can't

(GRAHAM *kisses* POLLY *again. They kiss, and then, she shifts so that her head is in his lap, legs hanging out the car window.*)

POLLY: I miss my boyfriend.

GRAHAM: You have a boyfriend?

POLLY: No. Not right now. But if I did, I'd miss him. I miss that thing of being close. You know? Just being close. I've been away from that for so long. What is the opposite of away?

GRAHAM: The opposite of away is here. *(Beat)* I can't believe you forgot I existed.

POLLY: Tell me about Anita. I don't remember her much. Just that she was there.

GRAHAM: We're a good couple.

POLLY: You said that already.

GRAHAM: It's true. We make sense.

POLLY: So why don't you feel loved?

GRAHAM: I don't know. *(Beat)* Why don't you?

POLLY: I don't know.

Scene: Long distance from the Days Inn Or, End Days at the Inn of Days

GRAHAM: The funeral was good.
As good as those things can be.
No one came.
His friends were all dead.
So it was small.

You know who showed up?
Remember Dad's third wife?
No. Not her, she didn't show up, she's dead, But –
remember her daughter?
That's right. Her.
No. I have no idea what she was doing there—
But there she was.
At Dad's funeral.
There she was.

Scene: Very messy transgressive I can't do this at home sex

POLLY: Have you noticed that very conservative people
cheating on their very conservative spouses seem to go
in for this very messy "I'm breaking all the rules kind
of transgressive talk dirty to me" sex? Not that I know
a lot about these things; I'm just saying.

Okay, and plus, there was this whole quasi-incest
factor even though we're not related—and that made
it—you know, that was—

And of course, his father had just—died.

NO. I'm not going to see him again.

Oh come on.

What good is it to be single and liberated if you can't
go back to the lame-ass Midwestern town you ran
away from once and sleep with your married ex
stepbrother? In a car.

And sometimes, and I know you know this, sometimes
we are able to see into the heart of another person,
into their very inner-most secreted heart,
and touch them there and set something into motion,
and, why not? Why not do that when we can? Why
not?

I've never mentioned him before?
Oh. He's the son of my mom's second husband,
the mean drunk one.
Right. Him.

No, I am not going to see him again.
I mean, Mundelein? What the hell is that?
Libertyville? What the hell is that?
I am not going to see him again.
No, no, no, no, no.

Scene: The motel. Later that night.

POLLY: How did you know where I was staying?

GRAHAM: I followed you home.

POLLY: You what?

GRAHAM: I wanted to make sure you got back safely.

POLLY: You followed me home?

GRAHAM: We do it all the time with the kids. Especially now that Cat's driving.

POLLY: That's creepy.

GRAHAM: It's parental.

POLLY: Creepy.

GRAHAM: But you like it.

(GRAHAM *kisses* POLLY.)

POLLY: Graham

GRAHAM: I like the way you say my name. The way you said it in that restaurant. I want to get closer to your mouth. I want to touch your mouth. I really just want to touch your mouth.

POLLY: Okay.

Scene: Can we float like this forever?

(GRAHAM *and* POLLY *in bed, late that night. He is awake. She is asleep. She wakes up.*)

GRAHAM: What if this were a raft?

POLLY: This is a bed.

GRAHAM: But what if it were a raft?

POLLY: We'd float.

GRAHAM: How long could we float?

POLLY: Not long.

GRAHAM: What if we could stay like this? Floating?

POLLY: Then it would have to be a fort. You can stay in a fort. It's safe. A raft is in danger. You can't stay on a raft.

GRAHAM: But what if we could? For a very long time. Just floating.

POLLY: No.

Scene: New York City, Alone.

(POLLY *returns to her life. She opens the door to her New York apartment and turns on the lights. No one is there. She likes it that way.*)

(POLLY *sits at her table.* POLLY *opens her mail.* POLLY *stands up.* POLLY *smiles.*)

Scene—This is Nolita

(*New York City 10 days later.* POLLY's *apartment in Nolita. She opens the door to* GRAHAM.)

POLLY: What are you doing?

GRAHAM: I'm on an odyssey.

POLLY: So what are you doing?

GRAHAM: Let me in.

(POLLY *does.*)

GRAHAM: So this where you live.

POLLY: This is Nolita.

GRAHAM: Who's "Nolita"?

POLLY: Where I live. The neighborhood. It's called Nolita. It used to be sweet, back in the day.

GRAHAM: What day?

POLLY: The past.

GRAHAM: Oh. Kiss me.

POLLY: Did you drive?

GRAHAM: I drove.

POLLY: Where did you park?

GRAHAM: The lot

POLLY: The lot's expensive.

GRAHAM: Don't worry about it. Kiss me.

POLLY: Have you been home? Since the funeral?

GRAHAM: I got close. To being home. and then, I kept going. And then I got here. Kiss me.

POLLY: What do you mean you kept going?

GRAHAM: *(Noticing—her tub in the middle of the kitchen)* What's that?

POLLY: My bathtub.

GRAHAM: What's it doing there?

POLLY: A lot of them are like this. The older apartments. They were built as tenements, so they have all sorts of—you know, a lot of them have showers or bathtubs in the kitchen. They were—

GRAHAM: It's weird.

POLLY: *(correcting him)*

Charming. Why haven't you gone home?

GRAHAM: I don't know. This place is…Nolita.

POLLY: It *is* nice. And Mott Street has a lot of history. It's in all those Bowery Boy movies. And Horatio Alger books. Packed with the mythology of the orphan boy who recreates himself, raises himself up by the—

GRAHAM: I bet you love that.

POLLY: Why are you here?

GRAHAM: You want me to leave?

POLLY: No.

GRAHAM: So kiss me.

(POLLY *does.*)

POLLY: An odyssey, huh?

GRAHAM: I've never just taken off. Done things I
wanted to do without asking, telling, consulting,
planning. And I'm old. You think you're old? Because
I'm old.

POLLY: I don't think I'm old.

GRAHAM: You keep talking about "in the day" and
whatever—that's old.

POLLY: No, it's just that in New York, the
neighborhoods change, they change really fast. So
"back in the day" just means, when I moved here.
More than fifteen years ago. And I was fond of it the
way it was. Dollar fifty breakfast specials at the place
on the corner, Bella's, which used to be this really
sweet family owned diner with black and white
checkered floors, now it's Habana and the sign from
Bella's sits in some upscale mens retail boutque. But—

GRAHAM: Back in "the day"?

POLLY: Yes. I went there all the time. They knew me.
And now it's different. That's all.

GRAHAM: Seems like an okay neighborhood to me. I
mean, this is thriving.

POLLY: Okay. You're not from here.

GRAHAM: You're not from here.

POLLY: I am so.

GRAHAM: You are not. You're from where I'm from.

POLLY: Hardly. I lived in Libertyville Illinois for a total
of the five years that our parents were married. But
my mom and I were *from* somewhere else before that,
another state entirely, and then, we moved again, and
again, and I moved here when I was eighteen and

never left and I am more from here than anywhere. I have lived here longer than anywhere else and I am from here. Okay?

GRAHAM: Okay. Don't get bent out of shape or anything.

POLLY: I am not getting bent out of shape. I am just saying, you don't know what you're talking about. Want to start over? This isn't going very well. Be nice to me.

GRAHAM: I am being nice.

POLLY: No you're not. You're kind of being an asshole, and I don't understand why you're running away from your family. Lets start again.

GRAHAM: What?

POLLY: You go outside and knock, and I'll let you in and we'll start all over. It works, really.

GRAHAM: You want to start all over?

POLLY: Well, not like all over all over—not like, Hi I'm Polly Freed and I was your stepsister for five years but we're strangers to each other except we're not anymore because we fucked in a rental car (which, by the way, I returned without any sign of the night before) —but more like— So, wow, you're in New York. How was the drive? Want a cigar?

GRAHAM: The drive was fine. You have cigars?

POLLY: Yes. They're Cohibas. I smuggled them from Paris.

GRAHAM: I don't think you have to smuggle those. I think you could have just—you know, packed them and brought them home. Unless you plan to wrap them in metal and run them through the scanning device, I think you'd be—

POLLY: Do you want one?

GRAHAM: Sure.

(POLLY *goes to get cigars.* GRAHAM *takes her hand and tries to pull her to him or at least kiss her—she pulls away—*)

POLLY: Do you really not get the thing about the neighborhoods changing?

GRAHAM: Do you really think I'm an asshole?

POLLY: I don't know.

GRAHAM: I'm not an asshole. Actually, that's a lie. I am. I am an asshole.

POLLY: Your father was an asshole.

GRAHAM: My father was an asshole.

POLLY: He was horrible to my mother.

GRAHAM: It was mutual. Come here.

POLLY: Why?

GRAHAM: Because I can't stop thinking about the corners of your mouth.

(POLLY *goes to* GRAHAM. *Sits in his lap, he starts to kiss her arms. the insides of her arms. She tries to keep talking.*)

POLLY: You know. This isn't about me. This is grief. This is about your father.

GRAHAM: I hope not.

(GRAHAM *continues to kiss* POLLY. *She continues to talk, as if her talking self and her body self are not in cahoots.*)

POLLY: You think I can save you, but I'm not going to save you. I am not good at saving people. I always fail when I try. I can pull them out of the water, but I can't ever get them to stop drowning. Graham? Are you drowning, Graham?

GRAHAM: You haunt me. I do things that have nothing to do with you. But you're there. Under my skin. Not like anyone else. And we're not related. We weren't

even close when we were pretending to be related.
Come here.

(The command works. POLLY *does.)*

POLLY: But it's just for now. You know that right?

GRAHAM: Right. Just for now.

Scene:
Cat is a straight A student, a rad action girl

(Lights up on CAT. *Seventeen and earnest)*

CAT: I work very hard. I get A's in all of my classes.
I am on time for everything. For Everything. I work
harder than the boys but I don't get rewarded. I
hear there was this thing a long time ago called "The
Revolution" but my mom doesn't seem to know about
it. My mom is always exhausted. Church doesn't help.
My mom is on a lot of committees and medication. I
think my mom wants my dad to come home. My dad
went to see his ex-stepsister in New York and he never
came back. I don't know what he's doing there. I mean,
ex-stepsister? That's not even a real relation. Plus,
she's like, she's not, you know, she's not a Christian. I
think she must lead a very scandalous and potentially
exciting life even if it does not fall under the contract or
rubric or whatever of the Church of God. I went on the
Internet this morning and looked up this Polly Freed. I
know a lot about her. I am going to get my father back.
I am going to bring him home. Mom's in the bedroom
with the lights out again and everything's quiet and
sometimes, you just have to take matters into your own
hands. Do you know what I mean?

Scene: Polly has to open the bar

POLLY: Okay, here is a set of keys, and here is a map. Here is a street map, and here is a subway map. You will be fine. What do you like to do? Tell me what you want to see, and I'll give you directions.

GRAHAM: Go. I'll be fine. Go.

POLLY: Okay. But here is the map, and here is the subway map. And here is—okay, I'll write down a couple of neighborhood places I really like, places you can walk to. Café Gitane, Café Habana, Café Coloniale, Café Café, Lovely Day, Housing Works…oh yeah, and the muffin place. Will you be okay?

GRAHAM: I'll be fine.

POLLY: But do you know how to get around?

GRAHAM: On foot. I will be fine. I live in Ohio, but I'm not retarded. And I have been to New York City before. I will be fine. Go.

(POLLY *starts to go.*)

GRAHAM: Wait.

(POLLY *stops.*)

GRAHAM: What's the bar called?

POLLY: Home.

GRAHAM: What?

POLLY: Home.

GRAHAM: Why?

POLLY: Why not?

GRAHAM: Because you want one?

POLLY: That's too easy. So here are directions.

GRAHAM: Home.

POLLY: Yes. Don't read into it.

GRAHAM: Okay.

POLLY: Meet me there later?

GRAHAM: Home.

POLLY: Stop saying the fucking name of the fucking bar.

GRAHAM: You are a very complicated girl. Woman. Whatever.

POLLY: I've been told. So here are directions. Don't get lost.

(POLLY *goes. Stands outside the door a moment. Just breathing. Rests herself against something and stands a moment. Takes a breath. Goes to the bar)*

Scene: Cat on the Amtrak. All Aboard.

CAT: The Amtrak is an amazing way to travel. All Aboard. You see the country, really you do. I don't have my own car, and air travel is expensive and also, lately, uncomfortable and dangerous. But this feels just fine. On the train. In the Club Car. Meeting people and listening to them talk. I could listen to people talk all day. Really, I could. And they have these stories, and they are. Dying. To talk. To tell you things. Everyone. So this is good. I arrive tomorrow. And in the meantime, big windows, strangers, the Oreos and seltzer I brought from home, and the way the land keeps changing. This is amazing. The way it changes. Have you ever just watched it change? Next stop...next stop...next stop... And he'll be waiting for me. My dad. He just needs someone to tell him where he lives.

Scene: The bar after hours

GRAHAM: I like this place.

POLLY: Thank you.

GRAHAM: It has character.

POLLY: Thank you.

GRAHAM: It's not one of those twelve dollar drink girls in short dresses bars. Are your drinks twelve dollars?

POLLY: Just the twelve dollar ones.

GRAHAM: And I liked watching you work. Now that you're closed, I can tell you, I liked watching you work.

POLLY: Oh yeah?

GRAHAM: Oh yeah. It was hot.

POLLY: Guys always say that.

GRAHAM: Don't.

POLLY: What?

GRAHAM: That— Guys always—don't say that.

POLLY: Sorry.

GRAHAM: It's—cavalier.

POLLY: Are you drunk?

GRAHAM: Yes!

(POLLY *smiles. Then notices*—GRAHAM *has discovered a picture of her mother over the cash register. He looks at it. She watches him looking.*)

GRAHAM: That's your mom.

(POLLY *nods.*)

GRAHAM: She looks happy.

POLLY: Yeah.

GRAHAM: I never saw her look like that.

POLLY: It was a rare occurrence.

GRAHAM: She wasn't happy with my dad.

POLLY: No one was happy with your dad.

GRAHAM: Do you miss her?

POLLY: *(Unsentimental, unapologetically)* Yes. But I miss her like something I never had. Besides, I left. Do you miss your mom?

GRAHAM: All the time.

POLLY: When I was a little girl, I used to talk to her, your mother. I thought her ghost was in our house.

GRAHAM: I am sure that it was.

POLLY: Her clothes were in the attic. When my mom and I moved in. They had big fights about it. Your dad wouldn't get rid of your mom's clothes until my mom made him.

GRAHAM: Your mom made him, and he made me. Come over. Go through her things. He couldn't touch her things. He made me do it for him.

POLLY: I don't remember that.

GRAHAM: You were probably at school.

POLLY: We hated that house. My mom always did. She called it "the Embassy." She called us "the hostages." She called your dad—

GRAHAM: Tell me about the good things. What was good?

POLLY: Nothing was good.

GRAHAM: Something was good.

POLLY: I remember fighting and yelling and screaming and broken things. Nothing good.

(GRAHAM notices the very top of a very pink thong, peeking out from POLLY's jeans,)

GRAHAM: What the hell is that?

POLLY: What?

GRAHAM: That. *(Pointing)* It's very pink.

POLLY: Oh.

GRAHAM: I can't get my wife to wear... *(...that)*. And I have tried.

POLLY: It sounds like you can't get your wife to do a lot of things. And I'm sure you have tried.

(Suddenly, GRAHAM seems upset. POLLY goes to him.)

POLLY: Graham?

GRAHAM: I want to miss him. But I don't.

POLLY: It's okay. I don't miss any of them.

Scene: Like a mother cat handles her young

(The middle of the night in POLLY's apartment. GRAHAM appears to be asleep.)

POLLY: I want to put my entire body in the space between your chin and the base of your spine. I want to fit my entire body underneath your chin, in the space that falls where your entire torso does. I want you to take the back of my neck into your mouth like a mother cat handles her young. I want you to bite the back of my neck and pick me up and carry me. For my own good. To keep me out of harm. To move me. Can you do that?

(GRAHAM opens his eyes. Watches POLLY a moment. Then closes them.)

Scene: Representing Anita

CAT: This is my mom. I mean, she's not here, but I'm going to pretend to be my mom for you because I feel that her presence is sorely missing. And I am here to "represent."

So. Here she is. Anita. Wife of Graham. Daughter of Henry and Susan. Mother of Catherine and two boy twins who are probably killing each other this very moment as we speak. Those twins. They have ADD and they're a mess. Anyway—

Anything you'd like to say to our nice friends on the Amtrak, Mom?

(CAT *as her mom*)

"No, honey. Just, you know. God loves you."

(CAT *as herself.*)

Well, yeah, Mom. DUH.
Mom didn't have anything to say.
Sorry. She's been quiet lately.

(*She rolls her eyes. Parents*)

Scene: Away on business

POLLY: We never talk about Anita.

GRAHAM: We talked about Anita in Mundelein.

POLLY: Sure. Before.

GRAHAM: And the other night in the bar.

POLLY: Well. We don't really talk about Anita.

GRAHAM: What do you want to know about Anita?

POLLY: I don't know. Nothing.

GRAHAM: I don't really want to talk about her.

POLLY: It's been two weeks. Do you call?

GRAHAM: I call.

POLLY: From my phone?

GRAHAM: From the cell.

POLLY: Does she know where you are?

GRAHAM: I live in a very conservative place.

POLLY: What does that mean?

GRAHAM: It means there are certain questions that do not get asked. Anita knows, I think she knows, I am somewhere I can ask.

POLLY: Ask what?

GRAHAM: Can I build you some shelves?

POLLY: That's not one of the questions.

GRAHAM: You're wasting a lot of space. Seriously. I was reading this article in one of your magazines. Like *Elle Décor* or something. About vertical space. I think you're ignoring your vertical space. You got a Home Depot in the neighborhood? I know it's not like, what you had in The Day, but I can't find a hardware store, and I have to pick up supplies. We can talk about all of that other stuff later. Is that okay? Can we talk about it later? Because right now, I'm a man with a mission.

POLLY: There is a hardware store North of here. Be careful with my vertical space.

Scene: Graham builds shelves

(GRAHAM *builds shelves.* POLLY *watches, amazed. She goes out. He finishes. He goes out. She comes in. There are shelves now.*)

Scene: Cat in the Club Car

CAT: I love Jesus Christ. I do. Seriously. Like someone
I know. They say "your own personal Jesus" and I can
find this, this thing of a Personal God. It's not like a
man, but also, kind of sometimes, Jesus feels like my
boyfriend who lives far away and who I have to love
from a distance but who always seems real close. Do
you know what I mean? Jesus is rad. Ohio is not rad.

Do you have a cigarette? I think I should start smoking.
I'm going to be eighteen next month. I think I want
to smoke when I'm eighteen. Just for a year or two
and then I will quit. I will get The Patch. Or the Gum.
Or be hypnotized. That'd be really neat, right? To be
hypnotized? But first, I have to start, and it's just for
a little while. So I can go through hypnosis later. And
the other thing, I need to kiss someone. I need to know
what that's like. Before Ohio State. Just once. I should
know. Right?

Scene: Plans for the improvement of Polly Freed

GRAHAM: Plans for the improvement of the life of Polly
Freed.

Does Polly have an I R A? Find out.
Shelves. (*Check.*)
Sand floors
Purchase pillows. (*Side-sleepers, down.*)
Upgrade all systems in Polly's technological life.
Hardware, software—investigate.
Digital camera. Persuade her to lose the archaic Pentax
thing
She thinks she likes the archaic Pentax thing; but she'll
love digital.
What else?
What else does Polly need?

Scene: The arrival of Cat

(POLLY *opens the door to...*)

CAT: Are you Polly Freed?

POLLY: Do you live in the building?

CAT: Not exactly. I have a complicated agenda. May I come in?

POLLY: Did someone buzz you in? Are you selling cookies? I'm sorry, I don't—

CAT: The door was open.

POLLY: Really? The front door? That's bad. The door is not supposed to be open.

CAT: The good Lord creates miracles where miracles are needed.
Nice shelves.

POLLY: Thanks.

CAT: I've come for my father. I know he's here. I'm Cat.

POLLY: Oh.

CAT: Yes. Time's up.

Scene: You must be hungry

(*In the apartment*)

POLLY: (*To* CAT) Would you like a cup of tea? Or some lunch? You must have traveling a long time. You must be hungry. Or thirsty. Or tired.

CAT: No thank you.

GRAHAM: Give her some tea.

POLLY: (*To* CAT) It has little jasmine flowers in it.

GRAHAM: What does?

POLLY: (*To* GRAHAM) The tea.

CAT: I don't think I like jasmine flowers.

GRAHAM: Take the tea.

POLLY: It's okay if she doesn't want tea.

CAT: I don't want tea.

POLLY: It's okay. *(Beat)* So. I have some things I need to do. Like laundry. I have to do laundry. And it's gonna take me a long time. So I'm gonna go. And you two can—you should—graham, if she wants anything, just—feed her. I'm sure she's hungry.

CAT: I'm not hungry.

GRAHAM: You don't have to leave. It's your apartment.

POLLY: No, no, no. I do. And it's okay. I have things to do. Like laundry and phone calls and things. *(To* CAT*)* You probably don't remember me, but I knew you a long time ago. And it's really great that you're here and make yourself at home. I mean that.

*(*POLLY *gathers her laundry and proceeds to kind of pull something together and drags it out of the room. This should be weird and theatrical. But finally, she is gone. And father and daughter are left alone.)*

GRAHAM: You're supposed to be in school.

CAT: I told them I'm doing an independent study.

GRAHAM: On what?

CAT: My father.

GRAHAM: What did you tell your mother?

CAT: I left her a very long note.

GRAHAM: A note?

CAT: It's more than you did.

*(*GRAHAM*—)*

CAT: Anyway, I talked to the boys and told them where I was going. And school doesn't care; it's second semester senior year. And you can learn a lot riding the train across America.

GRAHAM: You didn't go across America. You went from Ohio to New York.

CAT: And I learned a lot. Imagine if I'd traveled the whole country.

GRAHAM: How is your mother?

CAT: What do you care?

GRAHAM: I care.

CAT: Yeah, that's like apparent.

GRAHAM: Yeah. That is like, a parent.

CAT: Don't you think about us at all?

GRAHAM: Of course I do. I think about you all the time.

CAT: Does Mom know that?

(GRAHAM *doesn't answer.*)

CAT: Do you call?

GRAHAM: Yes. I call. I call. Why does everyone want to make sure that I am calling your mother!? I call. Okay? I call.

CAT: You didn't talk to me.

GRAHAM: Your mother didn't want me to.

(Beat)

CAT: She's doing that thing again where she stays up all night watching Home Shopping Network and playing online bingo. Which is not only gambling, but it is the Internet, which you know Mom has issues with. And the boys are—the boys are fine, I guess. They act like they don't care that you're gone, and whatever, maybe they don't. But people are starting to ask. So I just think you should come home. Don't you get it? How you have to come home now? We all think you've like left us for good or something and our otherwise happy family is entirely destroyed like people on T V, like those amoral dysfunctional family T V shows the left wing conspiracy likes to put out so they can sell music or whatever.

GRAHAM: Polly remembers the day you were born.

CAT: So!?

GRAHAM: She remembers my father. And I didn't really know her when our parents were married, when she was supposed to be my sister. I never knew her. I don't know how to explain this so that it sounds like anything that makes sense.

CAT: Because it doesn't! We have never met this person. We've never even *heard* about her.

GRAHAM: We weren't in touch.

(CAT—)

GRAHAM: But it's like she's pulling me out of the water. I didn't even know I was in the water until she started pulling me out.

CAT: Are you committing mortal sin with your stepsister?

GRAHAM: We're not related.

CAT: You know what I mean.

GRAHAM: I am not talking about these things with you.

CAT: Why?

GRAHAM: Because you are still the child, and I am still the parent, that is why.

CAT: I want you to come home with me. Are you going to come home with me?

GRAHAM: Call your mother and tell her where you are. Tell her you're with me. And tell her, tell her something that you think she'll understand.

CAT: She understands.

GRAHAM: Tell her anyway.

Scene: Cat in the apartment

POLLY: Here is a set of keys. And here is a map. Here is a street map and a subway map. You'll be fine. And here is the list I made for your father of neighborhood places.

CAT: *(Icily polite)* Thank you.

POLLY: New York is great. And it's all on a grid. So you won't get lost. And the list, the list has all these sweet little bookstores and coffee shops. Café Gitane, Café Habana, Café Colonial, Café Café, Lovely Day, Housing Works, um… there are more.

CAT: We won't be staying long enough for Café Café.

POLLY: Okay.

CAT: Do I sleep on the couch?

POLLY: Yes. And that sounds like it's not nice, but really it's very nice. Sometimes I sleep on the couch. I'll give you the quilt. You'll love the quilt. *(Beat)* I'm not keeping him.

CAT: Sure.

POLLY: He showed up. I didn't invite him. I didn't even call.

CAT: Where's he sleeping?

POLLY: Well.

CAT: Right.

POLLY: *(Careful with her)* How do you feel about that?

CAT: It's a sin. On more than one level.

POLLY: That is probably true.

CAT: It's true.

POLLY: I held you. When you were a baby.

CAT: I don't remember that.

POLLY: No. I didn't think you would.

CAT: My mom's the one who called and left you the message about the funeral.

POLLY: What do you mean?

(CAT *shrugs.*)

POLLY: That was your mother?

CAT: She thought it was the right thing to do.

POLLY: How did she find me?

CAT: Mom's like that. Mysterious ways.

POLLY: Oh.

CAT: She thought you should be there.

POLLY: Oh.

CAT: But I don't think she thought it would be like this.

POLLY: Where is your father?

CAT: In the car.

POLLY: What do you mean in the car?

CAT: That's where he goes.

POLLY: What do you mean where he goes?

CAT: He's been doing it all year. He sits in the car in the dark in the middle of the night. He's not trying to kill himself—I know because I have checked to make sure nothing's on. It's just something he's been doing. I don't know why.

POLLY: Oh. Sometimes people feel sad, and it's just sadness. And it doesn't mean anything. And it isn't bad. And it isn't even personal. And it clears us out so good things can come in later. And maybe what's going on with your dad is like that. Like the good kind of sadness. The kind that makes us ready. Do you know what I mean?

(CAT *shakes her head. Yes. and then, no.*)

(POLLY *nods.*)

POLLY: Right. Well. I'll go get pillows. And the quilt. The quilt is really nice.

CAT: Hey. There are degrees. Of sin. Like, if the two of you are sleeping in one bed the way we used to on big family trips when Mom and Dad would put all the kids in one bed… If it's like that…or if it's like…a long time ago in the prairie when pioneers went West settling the land and killing innocent people, I think they probably all slept in the same bed a lot, whole families, or like, when whole families have to live in one room, because you know, it's the prairie or like your ancestors did in tenement houses in New York City—if it's any of those things, you're probably okay. Is it any of those things?

(POLLY *shakes her head no.*)

CAT: I didn't think so.

(POLLY *leaves the room and comes back with the quilt. She puts on her shoes and leaves the apartment.*)

Scene: We can't have sex anymore

(GRAHAM, *in the car, in the expensive parking lot.* POLLY *knocks on the car window. He lets her in. She sits down next to him. Silence*)

POLLY: We can't have sex anymore.

GRAHAM: Why?

POLLY: Because your daughter's here.

GRAHAM: Not all the time. I mean, she'll go out and stuff. That's how Anita and I did it when the kids were—they go out. And then, when they're out, you just have to like seize the moment. So I know it's not spontaneous. But, you do what you can.

POLLY: I am not talking about the logistics of lovemaking.

GRAHAM: Oh. Then what are you talking about?

POLLY: Your teenaged daughter is sitting in my apartment worried about you.

GRAHAM: Why's she worried about me?

POLLY: Why are you sitting in the car?

GRAHAM: I'm thinking.

POLLY: What are you thinking about?

GRAHAM: Do you remember what happens in *The Odyssey*? I never read it.

POLLY: Something about sirens. I don't know.

GRAHAM: What's a siren? Is that like a mermaid?

POLLY: They lure sailors to their death.

(GRAHAM, yeah?)

(They sit in the car a moment.)

POLLY: He hangs out with a nymph.

GRAHAM: Who does?

POLLY: Odysseus. The hero of the Odyssey.

GRAHAM: A nymph?

(And then, like a bedtime story)

POLLY: Odysseus comes to her island. And stays. For a long time. And then he goes home. And, her name is Calypso. Like the name of the pink store across the street. Across the street from me. The store is really

called that. And a few doors down, Calypso Bijoux.
And Calypso Bebe. For jewels and babies. And, I swear
to God, down the street, Calypso Home. So. That is
what happens to our hero. Odysseus. On his Odyssey.
Before he goes home. To his wife. Who is named
Penelope.

GRAHAM: We don't have to have sex.

POLLY: We don't.

GRAHAM: Okay.

POLLY: Good.

(GRAHAM *and* POLLY *do anyway.*)

Scene: The next day

(CAT, *with her maps from* POLLY, *at a sidewalk café in
Nolita.*)

CAT: Dear Mom,
There are things I'd like to tell you about New York.
But I know you don't check email even though the
boys keep trying to show you how to use it. So. Here is
a postcard of Ground Zero and a lot of love. Which is
all that fits on this tiny space. —Cat

Dear Eddie and Robert,
I'm in New York with Daddy and his ex-stepsister, this
single, bar-owning, wine-drinking, jasmine-flower-
collecting Jewess named Polly Freed. I don't know
how I feel about it. She's okay. I guess. She's been
trying really hard to make me like her, and I haven't
yet decided if I will. But New York's cool. There are
all these sidewalk cafes and little shops and this funky
Cuban kind of place where very fashionable people
drink café con leche and eat corn. There are people
who speak all kinds of languages here, on every street,
and I could fall in love with it, only I can't because

I have to get Daddy to go home. Take care of Mom, okay? I know it freaks you both out when she gets all Apocalyptic and all, but just be nice to her and listen and make it easier for her if you can. She likes macaroni and cheese. You can make the cheap stuff from the box, and I bet she'll eat it. I'll be home soon. —Cat.

Scene: Stolen treasure booty

(POLLY *enters the apartment. She's by herself. She checks to make sure* CAT *and* GRAHAM *are both gone. She rummages through a drawer and reveals—as if it is stolen treasure booty—a very old baby doll. She lies down on the couch and places the baby on top of her body like it's a real baby and she holds it. She lies there with the baby doll for a little while. Then, she puts it back in the drawer and leaves the room.)*

Scene: What it was like

CAT: I don't understand.

GRAHAM: Well. It wasn't good.

POLLY: Ever. It wasn't ever good.

GRAHAM: It wasn't good with *my* mom either. But that was different. She was my mom.

POLLY: He married my mom, and we spent our first Christmas—

GRAHAM: As a "family"—

POLLY: At the Playboy Club.

CAT: The what!?

POLLY: In Lake Geneva.

GRAHAM: Wisconsin not Switzerland.

POLLY: I told my mom I wanted to be a bunny, and she sent me back to the room without room service privileges.

GRAHAM: I don't remember that.

POLLY: They used to fight a lot.

GRAHAM: A lot.

POLLY: My mom and his dad. Not the bunnies.

GRAHAM: I loved those bunnies.

CAT: EW.

POLLY: Who didn't?

CAT: EW.

POLLY: The bunnies were perfect. The bunnies had good outfits and didn't fight. Our parents fought. Even in the beginning. They always fought.

GRAHAM: Yes they did.

POLLY: We did too.

GRAHAM: Yes. We did too.

POLLY: Your dad called me names.

CAT: What kind of names?

POLLY: Mean ones.

GRAHAM: I'm sure they were better than what he called me.

POLLY: There was this one fight, he called me a "hussy" …Which was technically inaccurate because I was nineteen before I even kissed anyone!

CAT: Nineteen!?

GRAHAM: You know, I bet the bunnies fought.

POLLY: I bet they did.

CAT: This is all very strange.

GRAHAM: My wife and I don't fight.

CAT: No. But you get quiet. Getting quiet is just as bad.

POLLY: It's all bad.

CAT: It is.

GRAHAM: I don't get quiet. Your mother gets quiet. I get, I get—

CAT: You sit in the car.

GRAHAM: I sit in the car.

POLLY: Was he violent with your mother?

GRAHAM: Who knows? My mother was always drunk.

CAT: I have never heard these things.

GRAHAM: I don't talk about them. When I met your mother, it was like, when I met your mother, I thought, now (finally) things will be normal. Things will stay in place. No one will be drunk or crazy or mean or throw things—

POLLY: Or—for me—with the bar—they are loud and drunk and throwing things, but I'm the one in charge.

GRAHAM: And for me, quiet. They are quiet. People sit in the car.

CAT: For a long time.

GRAHAM: To think.

POLLY: They probably need to think.

GRAHAM: They probably do. There's so much to think about.

(GRAHAM *and* POLLY *exchange a look.*)

Scene: The impersonal floating sadness

CAT: So, I know you're sad. And I know it isn't personal.

GRAHAM: I don't know what you mean.

CAT: Polly said there's this impersonal floating sadness that doesn't belong to anybody.

GRAHAM: Is that what Polly said?

CAT: Yes. And I want you to know that I know, and it's okay.

GRAHAM: What's okay?

CAT: That you sit in the car in the middle of the night by yourself. And I've noticed, I mean, I know that you sleep through the night here and I also know that you don't do that at home. with mom. At home with mom. I also know that mom takes all those sleeping pills so you won't wake her up when you go wandering around the house.

GRAHAM: I don't wander around the house.

CAT: You do. You wake up and you wander and you go into the kitchen and you eat sometimes and you always end up in the front seat of the car, in your pajamas, like you're gonna go somewhere, only I know you're not going to go anywhere and I also know you're not trying to kill yourself because you don't turn the ignition on.

(GRAHAM *says nothing.*)

CAT: So I'm just saying, I know. Okay? I know. And it's okay.

GRAHAM: Okay.

CAT: And—I get why you like her. She's not like anyone at home.

GRAHAM: Polly knows what things feel like in the dark. In the car. By yourself.

CAT: Mom doesn't know those things.

GRAHAM: No. Mom doesn't know those things. But that's part of what I like about Mom. Mom doesn't feel like there's anything wrong.

CAT: Mom is starting to feel like something is wrong. Or haven't you noticed?

GRAHAM: You want to go to a museum?

CAT: What kind of museum?

GRAHAM: Any kind of museum. When I was your age, my mom and dad took me to New York, and we went to museums. (*Beat*) Lets not go to a museum. Lets walk.

Scene: Stolen treasure booty redux

(POLLY, *alone, takes the baby doll out of hiding again. Holds it. Then goes back to where she keeps her cigars. Lights one. Holds the baby doll and smokes a cigar*)

(*Key in lock.* CAT *enters.* POLLY *hurriedly puts the doll away and puts out the cigar.*)

CAT: Hey.

POLLY: Hey.

CAT: Were you smoking?

POLLY: A cigar. Want one?

CAT: No thank you.

POLLY: I don't smoke anything else. No cigarettes. No marijuana. I just like cigars. I'm not like, depraved or anything.

CAT: Okay. (*She heads towards her luggage.*) Where's my dad?

POLLY: He went to the hardware store. He wants to build something else. He's a little obsessed, if you ask me.

(CAT *and* POLLY *sit in silence. It's awkward.*)

POLLY: Can I get you/ are you hungry—?

CAT: //Can I ask you something?

CAT/POLLY: Sure.

(*Uncomfortable silence*)

CAT: I know everyone hated your mom, but she sounds okay to me.

(*Weird pause*)

POLLY: Is that what you want to ask me?

CAT: No. (*Beat*) I need your opinion.

POLLY: On my mom?

CAT: On, um, sex. I need sex advice.

POLLY: Oh.

CAT: And I know you know about that.

POLLY: I do.

CAT: You know how you said this thing yesterday about, you said this thing about when you were um, hadn't been kissed before? And it made me think, it made me think, okay, if I have a boyfriend, is he supposed to want to kiss me? Because he doesn't. And I think there's something wrong. With me. Is there something wrong with me?

POLLY: Of course not! Do you want to kiss him?

CAT: I think so.

POLLY: And what happens when you try? Do you try? Do you…?

CAT: I send invisible X-ray signals, and he ignores them.

POLLY: You send signals?

CAT: The secret silent ones to make him kiss me.

POLLY: I don't know about these signals.

CAT: My mom says he respects me.

POLLY: Do you think he could be gay?

CAT: What do you mean?

POLLY: Are you sure he likes girls?

CAT: He's a Christian.

POLLY: Right. But are you sure he likes girls?

CAT: Well sure. I just think he's very shy.

POLLY: I'm sure you're right.

CAT: Do you think he's—??

POLLY: I don't know. It's certainly a possibility. It is one possibility in a sea of possibilities.

CAT: Why aren't you married?

POLLY: Oh. That's a very complicated question. With a long boring answer.

CAT: Didn't you ever fall in love?

POLLY: Oh yes. More than once. *(She smiles, fond memories.)*

CAT: Are you in love with my father?

(POLLY is speechless.)

CAT: You know what I think falling in love is like? I think it's going to be like how ice cream tastes when it hits your mouth. Sweet and creamy and cold and like it shocks you a little but then, it's so nice.

POLLY: That is exactly what falling in love is like. It's exactly like that.

Scene: The list of guilty pleasures

(GRAHAM *and* POLLY, *in one another's arms*)

GRAHAM: Air Supply.

POLLY: No way.

GRAHAM: Way. Your turn.

POLLY: Cigars.

GRAHAM: Slot machines.

POLLY: Fashion magazines.

GRAHAM: Sit-coms.

POLLY: Gawker.

GRAHAM: *(Confused)* Which is?

POLLY: Gossip.
(Ah. He gets it.)

GRAHAM: The personals.

POLLY: Really?

GRAHAM: Yeah, so—?

POLLY: You.

GRAHAM: Me?

POLLY: You are—for me—a very guilty pleasure. But not mine to keep.

GRAHAM: "Keep"?

POLLY: I didn't mean keep. I know I just said keep. But I didn't mean keep.

GRAHAM: Right.

POLLY: But if you wanted to…stay…

GRAHAM: Yes?

POLLY: Stay.

(Beat. Whatever it is, it's not the right answer. And POLLY
knows it immediately.)

GRAHAM: When?

POLLY: Whenever.

GRAHAM: Oh. *(Beat)* I can't stay.

POLLY: I know.

GRAHAM: I can't.

POLLY: I know.

GRAHAM: You said he goes home. At the end. To
Penelope. You said it. He goes home.

POLLY: Yes. He does. *(Changing gear)* I should go to the
bar.

GRAHAM: Now?

POLLY: Yes. Yes, I have to…now. I um, I have—things.
A new employee. And no one really knows how to
close except me. They need me. So, I have to go.

*(*POLLY *gets out of bed and gets dressed.* GRAHAM *watches
her.)*

GRAHAM: Hey. How long did he stay on the island?

POLLY: I don't remember. *(Now, dressed, she goes.)*

Scene: Something rad

(Late at night, POLLY'*s.* CAT *enters—)*

GRAHAM: Where have you been?

CAT: The park.

GRAHAM: What park?

CAT: Washington Square. I met some skaters.

GRAHAM: Do you know what time it is?

CAT: It was very safe. And the skaters were totally watching out for me.

GRAHAM: What are you wearing?

CAT: It's Polly's. Like it?

GRAHAM: No.

CAT: Why not?

GRAHAM: I don't know. We're going home.

CAT: Now? it's really late. Where's Polly? I have to tell her something rad.

GRAHAM: What do you have tell her?

CAT: Just something rad about the skaters. I watched them for hours and they are not like the twins or the boys at home. They are virtuoso.

GRAHAM: They are what!?

CAT: It's Italian for "really good." Oh—and we ate flan, and don't tell Mom, I smoked a cigarette. But just one drag. And just a cigarette. It is totally *not* a gateway. And—they know so many things, the skaters. They know how to balance and leap and fly and—

GRAHAM: You smoked a cigarette?

CAT: Just one drag.

GRAHAM: Great. Great. Well, Polly's at the bar. So. Go on. Go tell her. Go to the bar. Have a shot. And tell her goodbye because we're leaving tomorrow.

CAT: I promised the skaters I'd be back tomorrow.

GRAHAM: Well, you will not be back tomorrow and the skaters will just have to survive.

CAT: Are you okay?

GRAHAM: I am not okay. I am very upset that you were smoking.

CAT: I don't believe you. Want some of her tea? I like that stuff with the jasmine flowers. I didn't think I would. But I do.

GRAHAM: Fuck.

CAT: Language.

GRAHAM: FUCK. FUCK. FUCK. I have to go to the bar.

CAT: Right now?

GRAHAM: Right now. I have to get Polly. She's at the bar. I have to go to the bar and get Polly.

CAT: Lets go.

GRAHAM: Without you.

(GRAHAM leaves. CAT waits a moment.)

(Then she gets her jacket and leaves, just after him, back to the Park.)

Scene: Saying goodbye

(Outside the bar, GRAHAM and POLLY make out against a wall.)

POLLY: It's just that…I didn't…

GRAHAM: Ssshhhhh.

Scene: You skate like a poem

(CAT watches the skaters in Washington Square Park.)

CAT: Hello. I'm Cat.
I've been watching you skate for the last two days.
You're good.
You know that?
What's your name?
Really? Shut. UP.
That. Is. So. Rad.

Jesus Martinez,
watching you skate is like watching a poem.

And I have never been kissed—I know, I know, I'm
almost eighteen. We start later where I come from.
Ohio.

(She mimes this like, O-waving HI- O.)

We do things differently there. But listen—

My friend Polly thinks my boyfriend might be gay, but
he's not *really* my boyfriend, he's just this boy I watch
movies with and see at Church so he might be "gay" I
don't know, but the thing is, I was thinking, it would
be wonderful to receive my first kiss from a boy named
Jesus who can skate like poems. Would that freak you
out? My mom says boys don't like girls who speak
their mind, but sometimes I just can't help speaking
mine. It's just something I kind of do. So. Want to kiss
me? And then you can go back and skate some more
and I can just like, sit here and watch you and draw
pictures and then, I'll go home. How do you feel about
that? It'd be kind of playing make-believe. So.

Want to?

Scene: Nothing left to say

*(GRAHAM, in his coat, carrying some kind of plastic bag full
of things, goes. POLLY watches.)*

*(Neither can say anything. There's nothing really to say.
They can barely look at each other.)*

(He goes. She is left alone.)

(Silence)

*(She feels like something inside of her will explode or implode
or fall out)*

(She sits on the floor.)

(She moves to the bathtub in the middle of the room and sits there.)

(Like a feral animal, she huddles in a corner in the bathtub.)

(She waits for him to come back.)

(He doesn't come back.)

(She gets out of the bathtub and pours herself a glass of water.)

(She gets back into the bathtub and drinks water.)

(She gets out again and gets the baby doll and her cigars and gets back in. She lights a cigar and smokes it in the bathtub. She waits for something to happen. It doesn't happen.)

(She puts the doll and the cigar down.)

(She becomes very still.)

(She pours herself another glass of water from the bathtub faucet. Drinks it.)

(The light changes, into something brilliant, and she smiles.)

POLLY: Oh.

(Lights out)

END OF PLAY

CPSIA information can be obtained
at www.ICGtesting.com
Printed in the USA
BVHW01s1342291117
501547BV00012B/243/P